Written and
Designed by
Mia Hay

Illustrated by
Sasha Izmaylova

Edited by
Heidi Cook

From Paw To Tail Creations

Presents

The Curious Case of Croc's Crunch

An Adventure with The Nile Crocodile
&
The Egyptian Plover Bird

Written and Designed by
Mia Hay

Illustrated by
Sasha Izmaylova

Edited by
Heidi Cook

Mr. Crocodile _Loved_ to eat.

His absolute favourite treat was Toffee Crunch.

Mr. Crocodile could eat Toffee Crunch for breakfast, brunch, lunch, and tea.
Toffee Crunch was **Gooey** and **Chewy** and **CRUNCHY** and **MUNCHY.**

It was ever so yummy, especially after melting in the heat.

One day, Mr. Crocodile lounged next to Freshwater Lake.

And while he lounged, he ate his favourite treat: Toffee Crunch.

TOFFEE CRUNCH
Little did he know that one bite would change
EVERYTHING.

"OUCH!" exclaimed Mr. Crocodile, clutching his jaw.
"Oh, this is not good, this will not do at all."
He tried to dislodge the offending chunk with his claw.
He couldn't reach far enough into his
mouth.
The treat was stuck in between
two teeth.

"Who will help me?" Mr. Crocodile moaned.
In the distance, he could see a Large
silhouette.
"Oh thank goodness!" he thought.
"I won't lose hope, just yet."

It was the strong and mighty Mrs. Hippopotamus.
"Maybe you could help me, Mrs. Hippopotamus?"
asked Mr. Crocodile.

Mrs. Hippopotamus roared,
"I will run along. I will **NOT** be your breakfast!"

Mr. Crocodile noticed Mr. Zebra nearby.
"Please, will you help me?" asked Mr. Crocodile.
RUSTLE
RUSTLE
SNAP

Mr. Zebra shouted,
"Don't try to fool me! It's not my fault you missed
your brunch!"

Since the land animals were not helpful,
Mr. Crocodile turned to the river turtle.

"Will you help unstick what is STUCK?"

splash

Ms. River Turtle mumbled,
"I know you already ate that munchy crunch, and
you will not have me for lunch!"

In the distance, a bright light gleaned,
Hopefully, this Porcupine will help his teeth be cleaned.

Porcupine stated, "I am honoured you would come to me."
"Though as you can see, you have disturbed my evening read."

The pain in Mr. Crocodile's tooth grew by the minute.
He thought with dread of having this toothache for
the rest of the week!
What if he could never eat anything again?
Mr. Crocodile whined,
"Why can't they just trust me more?"

Then Mr. Crocodile saw the littlest creature he had seen, so far.
Miss Plover Bird had perched in a tree and had seen everything.
"Oh, Miss Plover, would you be so kind as to help me, please?" Mr. Crocodile called.

The little bird looked shocked and hopped nervously.
"As long as you promise I won't become tea!"
she chirped.

Mr. Crocodile agreed,
"I promise this is no trick. Please be quick!"

Mr. Crocodile opened his mouth very **wide**.
Miss Plover Bird jumped gently into his mouth.
The Toffee Crunch was dislodged speedily.

" Ah, Finally!"
Mr. Crocodile sighed with relief.
"The toothache has passed."

Miss Plover Bird was equally relieved and
thankful there was no deceit.

She even agreed to continue cleaning his teeth.

Mr. Crocodile said,
"Thank you, Miss Plover!
You saved me from such great pain."
"I thought I might not ever be able to eat my
favourite treat, again!"

Themes

- To always tell the truth,
- It is okay to ask friends for help,
- Animal Science Subjects,
- The Hippopotamus, Zebra, River Turtle, and Porcupine are all prey of the Nile Crocodile in the wild,
- Moral-teaching stories using animal-based case studies:

The Nile Crocodile

Mutalism:

An action between two different animals, where something good happens for both.

The Egyptian Plover Bird

Symbiotic Relationship:

A friendship between two animals where the same event happens repeatedly.

ABOUT THE
Author

Mia Hay grew up in Devon, U.K. She has achieved Distinction Star in Level 3 Animal Management and Distinction in FdSc Animal Science. Her professional life took an unexpected turn after she left university to pursue a professional career. Working full-time in the Veterinary industry, she found her calling with writing and is carving her own path by setting up her own Writing and Illustration business: From Paw To Tail Creations.

She is following her dreams, going back to her artistic roots and using her knowledge to raise awareness of the wild Animal Kingdom. She is utilizing education and presenting it in a way that enables escapism and creativity. Her ultimate aim is to build worlds and universes that her readers can become engrossed in.

Visit From Paw To Tail Creations and follow her creative journey.

@FromPawToTailCreations   FromPawToTailCreations@gmail.com

ABOUT THE
Illustrator

My name is Sasha Izmaylova and I drew illustrations for this wonderful story. I've been working on it around 2 Autumn months and it feels like I had an exciting journey through Egypt and met all these lovely characters.

I am from Russia and I am a self-taught illustrator. I graduated as a teacher, but find myself into drawing. For now it's all for kid's literature. Probably because as a teacher I can imagine what children would like to see on pages of their favourite books. Growing as a professional I still love to experiment with forms and lines.

As Mr. Crocodile was looking for someone's help, I'm looking for new techniques to express the ideas. If you want to know more about me and my way as an artist, you can check my Instagram or e-mail me and I'll send you my portfolio. I would be glad to have new collaborations.

 @sasha_is_may    sashaizm96@gmail.com

The Official Colouring Book

Available on Amazon

RIGHT NOW

Order yours today!